National Incident Management System (NIMS) Supporting Technology Evaluation Program (STEP) Guide

April 2009

TABLE OF CONTENTS

LIST OF TABLES

LIST OF FIGURES

Cover Photo: Clanton, Alabama, 29 August 2005 - The FEMA Emergency Response Team (in balcony) work at the Alabama Emergency Operations Center. FEMA is monitoring Hurricane Katrina as it makes landfall on the gulf coast. FEMA/Mark Wolfe.

INTRODUCTION

This document is a comprehensive guide to the National Incident Management System Supporting Technology Evaluation Program (NIMS STEP). Evaluation activities are sponsored by the National Preparedness Directorate (NPD), Federal Emergency Management Agency (FEMA). This guide is designed to provide an orientation to the evaluation process and policies including vendor application requirements, product[1] selection methods, evaluation activities, and post-evaluation review/reporting processes.

> *"Systems operating in an incident management environment must be able to interact smoothly across disciplines and jurisdictions. Interoperability and compatibility are achieved through the use of tools such as common communications and data standards, digital data formats, equipment standards, and design standards."*
>
> *~ National Incident Management System*

Background

Homeland Security Presidential Directive (HSPD)-5 directed the Secretary of Homeland Security to develop and administer the National Incident Management System (NIMS). In 2004, the Department of Homeland Security (DHS) released NIMS to provide a consistent nationwide template to enable governments and responders to work together effectively and efficiently to manage incidents and planned events. Although the incident management framework can be adaptable to any situation, NIMS provides a standard structure and management concepts that transcend all incidents, including:

- Accountability
- Common Terminology
- Comprehensive Resource Management
- Information and Intelligence Management
- Integrated Communications
- Management Span-of-Control
- Modular Organization

> *"NIMS defines standardized mechanisms and establishes the resource management process to identify requirements, order and acquire, mobilize, track and report, recover and demobilize, reimburse, and inventory resources."*
>
> *~ National Incident Management System*

[1] The terms product, system, and technology are used interchangeably throughout this document.

- Unified Command Structure

> *"Emergency management and incident response activities rely on communications and information systems that provide a common operating picture to all command and coordination sites. NIMS describes the requirements necessary for a standardized framework for communications and emphasizes the need for a common operating picture. This component is based upon the concepts of interoperability, reliability, scalability and portability, as well as the resiliency and redundancy of communication and information systems."*
>
> *~ National Incident Management System*

The NIMS provides a framework and sets forth, among others, the requirement for interoperability and compatibility to enable a diverse set of public and private organizations to conduct well-integrated and effective incident management operations. Systems operating in an incident management environment must be able to work together and not interfere with one another. Interoperability and compatibility are achieved through the use of tools such as common communications and data standards. Establishing and maintaining a common operating picture and ensuring accessibility and interoperability are the principal goals of the Communication and Information Management component of NIMS.

The NIMS STEP supports NIMS implementation by providing an objective evaluation of supporting technologies – the use and incorporation of new and existing technologies to improve efficiency and effectiveness in all aspects of incident management. The Incident Management Systems Integration (IMSI) Division of NPD has tasked the NIMS Support Center (NIMS SC) to support and manage the day-to-day functions of the program.

The NIMS SC and the testing facility are located in Somerset, Kentucky. For additional information on the NIMS SC, refer to **Appendix C**. In 2008, the NIMS SC laboratory received accreditation by the American Association for Laboratory Accreditation (A2LA) for testing emergency response information technology. To achieve accreditation status, the laboratory was required to meet general requirements for the competencies of testing and calibration laboratories, as provided in International Organization for Standardization (ISO)/International Electrotechnical Commission (IEC) 17025:2005.

Recommended Standards

In 2007, IMSI Division identified and recommended that emergency management/response organizations and private sector vendors voluntarily adopt the following standards:

- American National Standards Institute (ANSI) InterNational Committee for Information Technology Standards (INCITS) 398-2005: Information Technology – Common Biometric Exchange Formats Framework (CBEFF).

- Institute of Electrical and Electronics Engineers (IEEE) 1512-2006: Standard for Common Incident Management Message Sets for Use by Emergency Management Centers.

- National Fire Protection Association (NFPA) 1221: Standard for Installation, Maintenance, and Use of Emergency Services Communications Systems.
- Organization for the Advancement of Structured Information Standards (OASIS) Common Alerting Protocol (CAP) v1.1.
- OASIS Emergency Data Exchange Language - Distribution Element (EDXL-DE) v1.0.
- OASIS Emergency Data Exchange Language - Resource Messaging (EDXL-RM) v1.0.
- OASIS Emergency Data Exchange Language - Hospital AVailability Exchange (EDXL-HAVE) v1.0.

These standards support a common operating picture, which requires the use of common interfaces among disparate communications and data management systems.

The Recommended Standards List (RSL) also includes two programmatic and incident management standards recommended by IMSI Division in 2006 – NFPA 1600: Standard on Disaster/Emergency Management and Business Continuity Programs (2007 Edition); and NFPA 1561: Standard on Emergency Services Incident Management System (2005 Edition).

From these recommended standards, NIMS STEP engineers test product's adherence to the CAP and Emergency Data Exchange Language (EDXL) suite of standards; however, engineers are conducting pilot tests for EDXL-RM and EDXL-HAVE.

Program Description

The purpose of NIMS STEP is to provide an objective evaluation of commercial and government software and hardware[2] products to assist in the implementation of the NIMS. Evaluation activities are designed to expand technology solutions and provide the emergency response community with an objective process to evaluate their purchases. Vendor participation in NIMS STEP is voluntary and the evaluation results and use of trade names in the report do not constitute a DHS or FEMA certification or endorsement of the use of such commercial hardware or software. The evaluations do not constitute a determination of NIMS compliance.

NIMS STEP has been designed to evaluate incident management-related software and hardware against NIMS criteria and NIMS technical standards. The NIMS criteria

[2] The term hardware is intended to relate specifically to products supporting the software under evaluation (e.g., sensors, cellular telephones, computer servers, etc.).

assessment is conducted by assessors with knowledge in the areas of emergency response and management and is qualitative in nature. The NIMS STEP team is comprised of recognized experts in the field of emergency management and response. Outreach efforts are made as part of the NIMS STEP Assessor Program to involve state and local emergency management officials and responders in the evaluation program (see **Appendix B**). Assessors use criteria derived from the NIMS document (December 2008). See **Appendix A** for a description of the assessment criteria. During the product selection and planning phase, the NIMS STEP team will determine if the product will be inspected against NIMS criteria. These criteria generally apply to products that are used during incident operations; however, there could be exceptions for certain types of products.

NIMS technical standard tests are objective in nature and based upon adopted standards. NIMS STEP engineers test vendor product's adherence to the CAP and EDXL-DE. If a product does not implement any of the technical standards, evaluators will review the product solely for NIMS concepts and principles. The NIMS STEP team is conducting pilot tests for the EDXL-RM and EDXL-HAVE standards in Fiscal Year (FY) 09. After completing a series of pilot tests, the evaluation program will formally expand to test products for their adherence to the EDXL-RM and EDXL-HAVE standards. Additional standards may be included in the program as they are approved by the IMSI Division.

The NIMS STEP has been designed to evaluate products that support emergency managers and responders in decision-making prior to and during an incident, such as the following types of products: (1) alert and warning systems (2) incident management; (3) communication and network infrastructure; (4) vulnerability analysis and consequence assessment; (5) intellegence and analysis; and (6) physical and cyber security, access control, and surveillance. Preparedness tools will be considered for an evaluation only if the vendor can demonstrate an operational capability to use the product during an actual incident or event.

Program Scope

NIMS STEP personnel evaluate products primarily in a controlled, simulated, Emergency Operations Center (EOC)-based environment. Some products require demonstration in a limited field setting. In these cases, the field setting is considered an extension of the laboratory environment. Evaluations take place typically over the course of one week during which recognized experts in the field of emergency management and response gain hands-on experience with the system. The team consists of objective evaluators, typically including one test engineer and at least three assessors for each product under evaluation. Engineers conduct technical analysis of a product's adherence to the standards under review. The assessors conduct qualitative analysis and provide feedback on the product based on concepts and principles from the NIMS document (December 2008). Input from the assessors is captured using a Dichotomous rating scale – a quantitative method for measuring the agreement or disagreement for a set of NIMS-related statements. These methods are designed to help describe products and to determine the presence or absence of desirable attributes.

Benefits to Vendors

NIMS STEP supports vendors in their implementation of NIMS and associated standards, concepts, and principles. Vendors will receive a copy of the evaluation report including feedback from end-user representatives and test engineers; these services are provided at no cost to the vendor. Vendors may use results of the evaluation to demonstrate with users their commitment to NIMS and the use of standards to maintain interoperability with other applications or platforms. The results of the test may also support the vendor in identifying areas for enhancement during future development of their product. The report will also identify the capabilities of the system as related to its incorporation of NIMS concepts and principles as well as the product's adherance to the CAP and EDXL suite of standards, if applicable. The results from each evaluation will be posted on the Responder Knowledge Base (RKB) (https://www.rkb.us/) website. The RKB website provides government officials and other end users with access to evaluated products and results.

Benefits to Emergency Management/Response Personnel

NIMS STEP supports practitioners in their decision making during the purchasing and procurement process. The primary benefits to Emergency Management/Response Personnel[3] include access to reports based on results from an objective evaluation. Practitioners can also utilize NIMS technical standards and criteria for reference when purchasing hardware and software off the shelf or in Requests For Proposals (RFPs) when developing new products.

Benefits to External Assessors

The NIMS STEP Assessor Program aims to involve state and local emergency management officials and responders in the evaluation program. Officials that participate as an assessor learn about new incident management technologies, and gain an understanding of interoperability standards and NIMS concepts for the benefit of their jurisdiction. Additionally, documentation of participation will be provided to assessors after the completion of an evaluation which will identify their participation as volunteer work. This document may be used to reach personal improvement goals.

---

[3] ***Emergency Management/Response Personnel:*** *Includes federal, state, territorial, tribal, substate regional, and local governments, private sector organizations, critical infrastructure owners and operators, Non-Governmental Organizations (NGOs), and all other organizations and individuals who assume an emergency management role. Also known as Emergency Responder. – National Incident Management System*

EVALUATION PROCESS

Figure 1, Evaluation Process Overview, provides an overview of the evaluation process. The following sections describe the application process, coordination between the NIMS STEP team and vendors, evaluation conduct, and the reporting process in more detail.

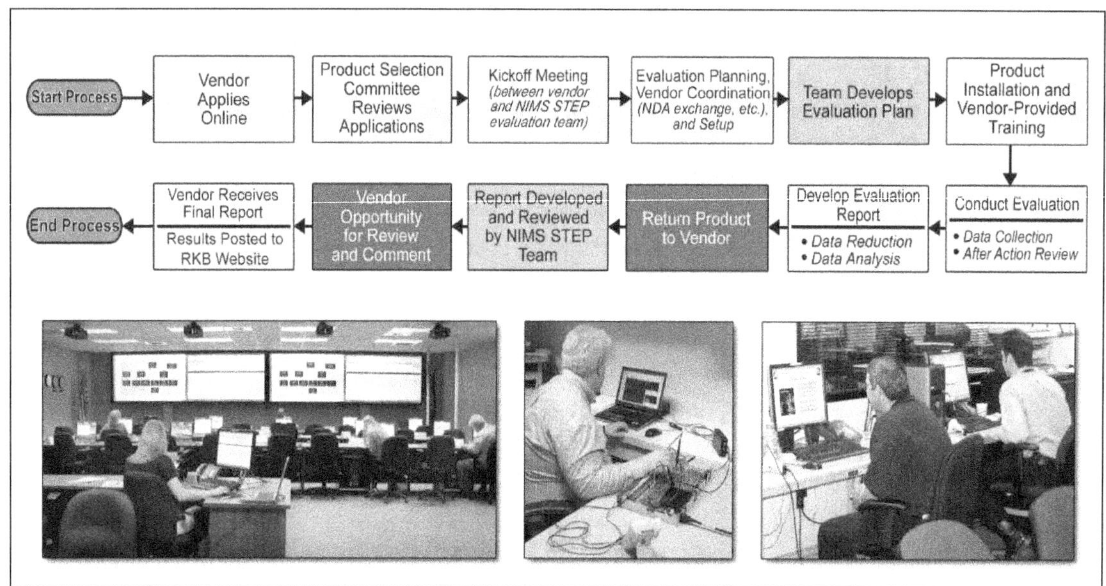

Figure 1: Evaluation Process Overview

Application Materials

Vendors are responsible for completing all application materials and submitting documentation to the NIMS STEP team. The vendor application materials are available on the program website (http://www.nimsstep.org) and vendors should submit their application for evaluation using the online system. The initial application should include *Vendor Application Part 1 – Intent for Evaluation* and supporting system documentation, as the vendor deems appropriate. A vendor self-assessment, consisting of a completed *NIMS STEP Worksheet* will be required during the application process (**see Appendix A Table A-2, NIMS STEP Worksheet**).

Product Selection

The program has established an objective process to select products for evaluation. Staff will review vendor applications based on the order they are received. Products will be reviewed for applicability to the program objectives and relevance to the emergency response and management community. NIMS criteria apply to products that are used during incident operations to assist in managing an incident. Products typically fall within one or more of the following categories:

1. Alert and Warning Systems: Supports warning the public and alerting responders to the presence of a particular hazard or critical event.

2. Incident Management: Effective and efficient response requires command, control, and communication from tactical on-scene locations to local and state EOCs, as well as Federal operations centers. The real-time delivery of critical information among responders, emergency management officials, and executives at all levels of government is critical. Among other products that support these goals, resource management applications assist organizations inventory, track and report, request and order, and recover resources.

3. Communication and Network Infrastructure: Communication between interconnected wired and wireless networks and commercial systems for voice, text, graphic, video, and spatial information, providing broad-based intelligence and highly-focused operational information.

Products applicable to NIMS STEP may also apply to one or more of the following categories:

4. Vulnerability Analysis and Consequence Assessment: Software that provides emergency management/response officials with information on natural and infrastructure risks, forecasts incident consequences, and/or analyzes the impact of hazards based on demographic data and human needs. These products lead to decisions and response activities and increase confidence among officials and the public.

5. Intelligence and Analysis: Products that support multi-source collection and the production and dissemination of intelligence to incident response organizations so they can monitor threats, detect and prevent attacks, and alert authorities.

6. Physical and Cyber Security, Access Control, and Surveillance: Products that support site monitoring, personnel identification and authentication, and the detection of physical and electronic incursions that are fully integrated and interoperable with responder systems and analytical decision-support tools.

In order to be considered for an evaluation, products must meet minimum requirements as identified in the Vendor Application. Specifically, priority will be given to products that have the potential to meet a need in the field based on a written request from an emergency manager or responder, implement one or more of the recommended technical standards (CAP, EDXL-DE, EDXL-RM, or EDXL-HAVE), have applicability to NIMS, are mature enough in their development for evaluation, and demonstrate an operational capability for use during an incident or event. In applying for the program, vendors should consider both their timetable for future product releases and the maturity of their product. Products must be deployed in the field and not in a development or prototype phase to be considered for the program. The NIMS STEP staff will review application materials, and schedule evaluations based on the availability of program resources. The evaluation team will notify the applicant of the status of their application and proceed with evaluation planning to include an initial call from a member of the staff and coordination of a Non-Disclosure Agreement (NDA).

Evaluation Planning and Setup

Once a product is selected for evaluation, a member of the NIMS STEP staff will contact the vendor to introduce them to the evaluation process, to answer any questions they may have about the program, and to initiate logistics coordination activities. During the initial planning phase, vendors will be asked to sign a *Vendor Consent Form* (**see Appendix E**) to indicate that they have read and agree to the policies outlined in this guide. Additionally, the program has an approved NDA process in place that will be coordinated with each vendor.

Vendors will be asked to complete supplementary vendor application materials once appropriate NDA and consent forms are in place. Upon receipt of supplementary application materials, staff will develop a timeline for conducting the evaluation and coordinate detailed logistics with the vendor to include product installation/web access, supporting software/hardware requirements, evaluator training, and technical support for installation and evaluation conduct.

In the event that significant technical or operational issues surface prior to the evaluation, the team will advise the vendor. The vendor will then have the option to perform corrective actions, begin the evaluation without taking corrective actions, or withdraw from the evaluation. The evaluation begins at the start of product installation/setup after which the vendor will not be permitted to withdraw their product from the evaluation process.

Evaluation Conduct – NIMS Concepts and Principles

Assessors inspect the product's incorporation of NIMS concepts and principles. The primary sub-elements of the NIMS portion of the evaluation are: Emergency Support, Hazards, Communication and Information Management, Resource Management, and Command and Management. Assessors also review general questions on the product including Implementation Considerations. All evaluators receive training on the product and review available system documentation and training materials. At the conclusion of training, assessors will work with the system during practical exercises and realistic scenarios to become familiar with system capabilities. After utilization of the system, assessors will complete a *NIMS STEP Worksheet* and document their observations (**see Appendix A**). Assessors will inspect products against established criteria to ensure they are consistent with NIMS concepts and principles. Certain criteria may not be applicable to all types of products and will be rated as Not Applicable (N/A). Assessors also provide qualitative responses along with their ratings. **Table 1,** NIMS Criteria Summary Table, provides a notional summary of key findings for NIMS elements.

Table 1: NIMS Criteria Summary Table (Notional)

NIMS Criteria	Consistent with NIMS? Agree / Disagree / Not Applicable
1. Emergency Support	
2. Hazards	
3. Communications and Information Management	
4. Resource Management	
5. Command and Management	

Evaluation Conduct – Adherence to Standards

This second portion of the evaluation addresses the implementation of standards. In FY09, the program has the capability to test the adherence of products to the following two NIMS standards: CAP v1.1 and EDXL-DE v1.0. The NIMS STEP team is conducting pilot evaluations for the EDXL-RM v1.0 and EDXL-HAVE v1.0 standards in FY09. Additional NIMS standards may be incorporated in the NIMS STEP in FY10. Applicable standards will be referenced on the website and in program documentation. The following sections provide a summary of each standard currently implemented in the evaluation program.

Common Alerting Protocol

The CAP is a simple but general format for exchanging all-hazard emergency alerts and public warnings over all kinds of networks. CAP allows a consistent alert or warning message to be disseminated simultaneously over many different warning systems, thus increasing warning effectiveness while simplifying the warning task. CAP also facilitates the detection of emerging patterns in local warnings, which may help officials identify hazards and initiate the appropriate response. The test cases for CAP are included in **Table 2, CAP Test Cases**. The first three test cases are specifically related to the CAP standard. The fourth test case is derived based on the intent of the CAP standard to facilitate interoperability and information sharing. For the purposes of the transaction test case (TEST_004), a disparate system is defined as a third party application or product (government or commercial). To successfully demonstrate transaction, the system under test must send/receive CAP messages (as applicable to the product) to a minimum of one disparate system. Test engineers provide a separate rating for sending and receiving. **Figure 2, CAP Message Test Process**, depicts the process for the four test cases. For additional information on the CAP standard refer to the OASIS website (http://www.oasis-open.org/home/index.php).

Table 2: CAP Test Cases

Test Case Identifier	Test Case Title	Test Objective
TEST_CAP_001	Generate CAP Alert Message	Generate a CAP Alert message for use in the eXtensible Markup Language (XML)/Schema validation, CAP conformance, and transaction testing.
TEST_CAP_002	XML/Schema Validation	Determine if the message is well formed and valid against a CAP 1.1 applied schema.
TEST_CAP_003	CAP Conformance	Determine if the CAP standard is applied in the correct format to include proper application of cardinality of elements, CAP standard structure, mandatory and optional elements, and conditional rules.
TEST_CAP_004	Transaction	Verify transaction (send and / or receive) with disparate systems.

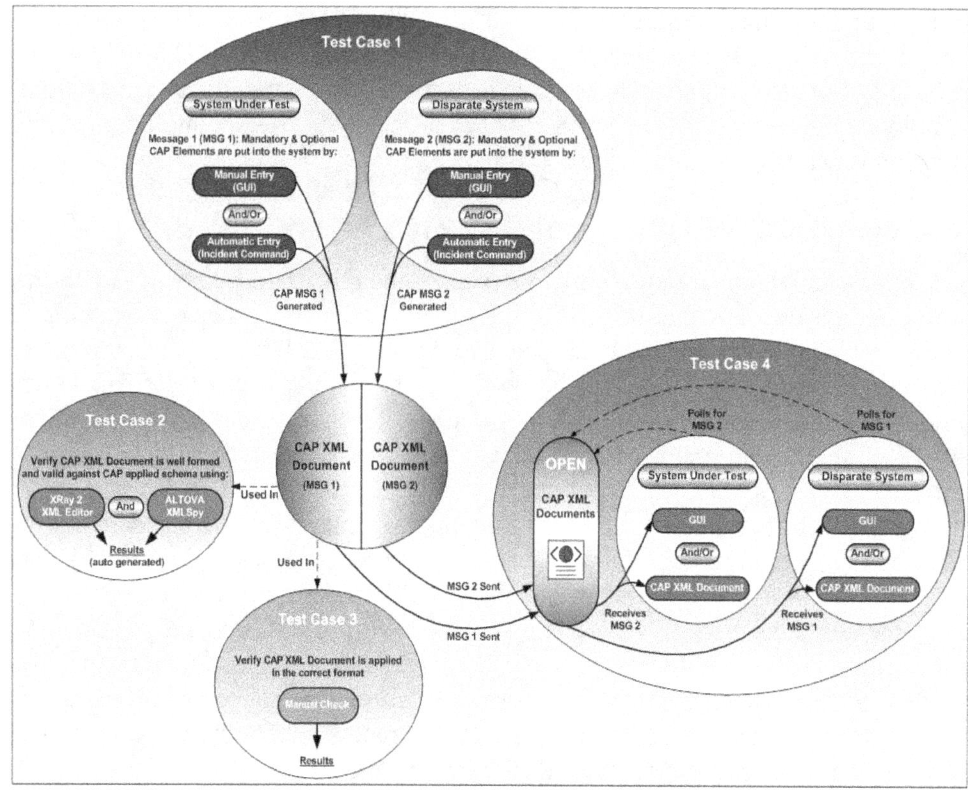

Figure 2: CAP Message Test Process

Notional results of adherance to specific standards may be reported in a summary format similar to that depicted in **Table 3, CAP Test Results (Notional)**. Products are judged on a scale as depicted below; they are not assigned an overall pass/fail rating. The items shown in bold negatively impacted the rating in that area. The other items provided are observations.

Table 3: CAP Test Results (Notional)

Legend:

▲ Meets requirements; no issues identified.

△ Partially meets requirements; minor issues identified.

▽ Partially meets requirements; major issues identified.

▼ Does not meet requirements.

○ No Rating or Not Applicable (N/A) to the system.

Test Case Identifier	Test Case Title	Rating	Key Findings
TEST_CAP_001	Generate CAP Alert Message	▲ Meets requirements; no issues identified.	This system can be used to develop CAP alert messages. Engineers successfully entered all required and optional elements. System provides a direct method to save and extract the CAP XML file.
TEST_CAP_002	XML/Schema Validation	△ Partially meets requirements; minor issues identified.	Minor issues were identified with the format of the CAP alert message content. Messages were well formed but **did not validate against the CAP 1.1 schema due to an incorrect date/time format.**
TEST_CAP_003	CAP Conformance	△ Partially meets requirements; minor issues identified.	Minor issues were identified with the conformance to the CAP standard. **The system did not use a proper date/time format for the <sent> element. Additionally, the <identifier> element included spaces.** Engineers confirmed the presence of all mandatory elements and proper cardinality of all elements. All business rules were properly implemented. Does not include optional elements include <Digest> and <Parameter>.

TEST_CAP_004	Transaction (send)	Partially meets requirements; minor issues identified.	Engineers sent CAP alert messages from the system under test to Disaster Management Interoperability Services (DMIS) using Open Platform for Emergency Networks (OPEN). **Due to the discrepancy with the date/time format, three optional elements (<effective>, <onset>, and <expires>) did not display properly when received by DMIS.**
	Transaction (receive)	Partially meets requirements; major issues identified.	**This system rejected incoming messages from DMIS. This problem was attributed to issues with the <derefUri> element.**

Emergency Data eXchange Language-Distribution Element

The Distribution Element specification describes a standard message distribution framework for data sharing among emergency information systems using the XML-based EDXL. This format may be used over any data transmission system, including the Simple Object Access Protocol (SOAP) Hypertext Transfer Protocol (HTTP) binding. For additional information on the EDXL-DE standard refer to OASIS website (http://www.oasis-open.org/home/index.php). The EDXL-DE test cases are structured in a format similar to the CAP cases. The test cases for EDXL-DE are included in **Table 4, EDXL-DE Test Cases**.

Table 4: EDXL-DE Test Cases

Test Case Identifier	Test Case Title	Test Objective
TEST_EDXL-DE_001	Generate EDXL-DE Alert Message	Generate an EDXL-DE message for use in the EDXL-DE XML/Schema validation, conformance, and transaction testing.
TEST_EDXL-DE_002	XML/Schema Validation	Determine if the message is well formed and valid against an EDXL-DE 1.0 applied schema.
TEST_EDXL-DE_003	EDXL-DE Conformance	Determine if the EDXL-DE standard is applied in the correct format to include proper application of cardinality of elements, EDXL-DE standard structure, mandatory and optional elements, and conditional rules.
TEST_EDXL-DE_004	Transaction	Verify transaction (send and / or receive) with disparate systems.

Notional results of adherance to specific standards may be reported in a summary format similar to that depicted in **Table 5, EDXL-DE Test Results (Notional)**. Products are judged on a scale as depicted below; they are not assigned an overall pass/fail rating. The items shown in bold negatively impacted the rating in that area. The other items provided are observations.

Table 5: EDXL-DE Test Results (Notional)

Legend:

▲ Meets requirements; no issues identified.

△ Partially meets requirements; minor issues identified.

▽ Partially meets requirements; major issues identified.

▼ Does not meet requirements.

○ No Rating or Not Applicable (N/A) to the system.

Test Case Identifier	Test Case Title	Rating	Key Findings
TEST_EDXL-DE_001	Generate EDXL-DE Alert Message	Meets requirements; no issues identified.	EDXL-DE messages were automatically generated based on modification of incident information.
TEST_EDXL-DE_002	XML/Schema Validation	Meets requirements; no issues identified.	EDXL-DE messages properly validated to the schema.
TEST_EDXL-DE_003	EDXL-DE Conformance	Meets requirements; no issues identified.	Messages properly conformed to the EDXL-DE standard.
TEST_EDXL-DE_004	Transaction (send)	Partially meets requirements; minor issues identified.	EDXL-DE messages were successfully sent to OPEN and a disparate system. **One optional element <senderRole> permitted multiple entries but the system only sent the first entry.**
	Transaction (receive)	No Rating or Not Applicable (N/A) to the system.	The product's primary purpose is to generate and send messages. It does not provide the capability to receive messages.

Data Collection, Analysis, and Reporting

The primary data collected during evaluations is one collective NIMS STEP Worksheet, and a set of completed test procedure logs for each standard (as applicable to the product). All participants submit observations electronically through the Test and Evaluation (T&E) Data Collection System (DCS) and participate in after-action reviews. Data analysis and Quality Control (QC) begin during the evaluation and conclude with the development of an evaluation report.

The evaluation team's report will include a description of events that occurred during the evaluation; results regarding NIMS elements and adherence to each of the identified standards; and references to product documentation. The report may also include participant observations and select comments/ratings from evaluation team members.

Vendors will have an opportunity to review a draft of the evaluation report within 45 working days after completion of the evaluation. The vendor has up to 10 working days to review the report and provide comments. After reviewing and addressing vendor feedback, the vendor will receive an updated copy of the report and have an opportunity to develop a response letter for inclusion in the final report. NIMS STEP staff will also develop a brief summary of the evaluation report.

Follow-on Testing

The vendor has the option to request a re-test when providing a response to the draft report. Follow-on tests are typically limited to products which did not meet the standards in one or more areas and that provide documentation to demonstrate that corrective actions have been completed. Re-tests will be scheduled based on resource availability and evaluation schedules. The original results will be submitted to the RKB website and the results of the re-test will supplement original findings. An application form for a re-test is provided online. If major system upgrades are performed; vendors will have the opportunity to resubmit their product for evaluation through the standard application process.

Program Websites

The vendor application materials are available on the program website and vendors should submit their application for evaluation using the online system (http://www.nimsstep.org). The website also addresses Frequently Asked Questions and includes a copy of this Guide. The results from each evaluation will be posted on the RKB (https://www.rkb.us/) website regardless of the outcome. By participating in the program, vendors provide their consent to the IMSI Division regarding the posting of the results for public viewing. The evaluation results and use of trade names on the program website do not constitute a DHS or FEMA certification or endorsement of the use of such commercial hardware or software. The evaluations do not constitute a determination of NIMS compliance.

Program Improvement

The evaluation program includes a process for soliciting and addressing feedback from vendors in order to ensure continuous program improvement. This includes a questionnaire for all vendors participating in the evaluation program. The NIMS Technology Evaluation and Standards Working Group and IMSI Division will review vendor comments and suggest changes to the program.

ROLES AND RESPONSIBILITIES

Table 6, Participating Agencies, outlines the roles and responsibilities of participating agencies.

Table 6: Participating Agencies

Organization	Roles and Responsibilities
National Preparedness Directorate	FEMA's NPD provides strategy, policy, and planning guidance to build prevention, protection, response, and recovery capabilities among all levels of government throughout the Nation. The IMSI Division of NPD oversees response policy by maintaining, revising, and disseminating the NIMS, the National Response Framework (NRF), and related materials. The IMSI Division directs and provides oversight of the NIMS STEP. They are also responsible for identifying standards for the NIMS STEP team to implement. Although removed from the evaluation itself, the IMSI Division will make final decisions about all program process matters.
National Incident Management System Support Center	The IMSI Division of NPD has tasked the NIMS SC to support and manage the day-to-day functions of the NIMS STEP. The NIMS SC and the testing facility are located in Somerset, Kentucky. The evaluation team consists of a test director, test analysts, assessors, test engineers, and Information Technology (IT) personnel. Evaluators adhere to a NDA and a code of conduct which ensures objectivity and the protection of company sensitive information. Assessors conducting the inspection of NIMS concepts and principles have extensive training and experience in emergency management and response and maintain updated knowledge regarding issues and practices in their discipline. Assessors may be generalists or practitioners within the field of emergency management and response. All assessors have a thorough understanding of emergency management principles and the concepts and principles of NIMS. Specifically, assessors will be required to meet minimum qualifications in the following areas: years of experience in their discipline (e.g., medical, fire, law enforcement), completed courses (e.g., Independent Study (IS)-100, IS-200), participation in responding to real-world incidents, and experience using software during exercises and/or real-world incidents. Test engineers will be qualified in a technical field and will be required to have demonstrated experience in their domain (e.g., electrical engineering, software test).
NIMS Technology Evaluation and Standards Working Group	The Technology Evaluation and Standards Working Group will be composed of approximately 10 practitioners and Subject Matter Experts (SMEs) familiar with information management standards and test and evaluation. The group will provide the IMSI Division and the NIMS STEP team with input regarding the application of NIMS standards in the program. For additional information on the working group including a summary of their roles and responsibilities refer to **Appendix D**.
Vendors	Vendors are responsible for completing application materials and, if selected, for training evaluators in a manner consistent with typical end-user training. Vendors will be required to provide evaluators with access to their system, and to provide technical support during system installation and product evaluation. Typically, vendors support evaluations on site with set up/installation and training; however, some products may be supported remotely.

APPENDIX A: NIMS INSPECTION CRITERIA

Purpose

This appendix has been developed to serve as a procedural aid to assessors reviewing a product for incorporation of NIMS concepts and principles. All assessors have a full understanding of the methodology that will be used in this inspection process and the proper application of the selected inspection criteria. This guide provides an overview of the methodology to be used in the inspection process as well as step-by-step instructions for conducting the inspection. The appendix specifically identifies and further describes the criteria to be used and provides assessors with instructions for completing the NIMS STEP Worksheet. Assessors are required to provide narrative explanations and general observations for select questionnaire responses.

Inspection Instructions

The results of the inspection process will be a description of the relevance of the product to the NIMS. This is accomplished by assessing how applicable each product is to Inspection Criteria from NIMS, as well as by addressing subjective questions related to each Inspection Criteria and the product as a whole.

The process includes three steps:

- *Step 1*: Review the Inspection Criteria.
- *Step 2*: Apply each Inspection Criteria to, and answer the questions for, the product.
- *Step 3*: Address the general questions to the product as a whole.

Step 1 – Review the Inspection Criteria

The Inspection Criteria was developed by a cross-section of SMEs and selected members of the emergency response community. Assessors inspect the product's incorporation of NIMS concepts and principles. The primary sub-elements of the NIMS portion of the evaluation are as follows:

- Emergency Support
- Hazards
- Communication and Information Management
- Resource Management
- Command and Management

Assessors also review general questions on the product including Implementation Considerations.

Assessors conduct qualitative analysis and provide feedback for all of the criteria listed above. Input from the assessors is captured using a Dichotomous rating scale – a quantitative method for measuring the agreement or disagreement for a set of NIMS-related statements. These methods are designed to help describe products and to determine the presence or absence of desirable attributes. **Table A-1, NIMS Criteria Summary Table,** is reflected below; assessors will complete this table for inclusion in each evaluation report.

Table A-1: NIMS Criteria Summary Table

NIMS Criteria	Consistent with NIMS? Agree / Disagree / Not Applicable
1. Emergency Support	
2. Hazards	
3. Communications and Information Management	
4. Resource Management	
5. Command and Management	

Additional descriptions associated with each inspection criterion are outlined below.

Emergency Support

The selected product should be applicable to Emergency Support Functions (ESF) and/or the Incident Command System (ICS). This is not to infer that a product cannot apply to a single category. Instead, it is intended to underscore a preference for product applicability across the greatest number of categories.

ESFs are defined in the NRF as:

- Transportation
- Communications
- Public Works and Engineering
- Firefighting
- Emergency Management
- Mass Care, Emergency Assistance, Housing, and Human Services
- Logistics Management and Resource Support
- Public Health and Medical Services
- Search and Rescue
- Oil and Hazardous Materials Response

- Agriculture and Natural Resources
- Energy
- Public Safety and Security
- Long-Term Community Recovery
- External Affairs

Incident Command Functions are defined in the NIMS document as follows:

- Incident Command
- Operations Function
- Planning Function
- Logistics Function
- Finance/Administration Function
- Intelligence/Investigations Function
- Public Information Function
- Safety Function
- Liaison Function

Hazards

Each product should mirror the all-hazards philosophy of NIMS to the greatest extent possible. Assessors review the product's applicability to the general categories of natural and manmade hazards, as defined by NIMS. The specific types of hazards identified in this section are from the NFPA 1600: Standard on Disaster/Emergency Management and Business Continuity Programs. The standard should be referenced for specific examples and detailed definitions. Following is a summary list of hazards for reference in the inspection of each product:

Natural hazards:

- Geological (earthquake, tsunami, volcano, landslide, etc.)
- Meteorological (flood, tidal surge, drought, forest fire, snow, windstorm, extreme temperature, etc.)
- Biological (emerging diseases [pandemic disease, West Nile virus, smallpox], Animal or insect infestation, etc.)

Manmade hazards:

Human-caused incidents

- Accidental (hazardous material spill or release, explosion/fire, transportation accident, building/structure collapse, air/water pollution, contamination, etc.)
- Intentional (terrorism [explosive, chemical, biological, radiological, nuclear, cyber], sabotage, civil disturbance, etc.)

Technological-caused incidents

- Technological-caused incidents (central computer, mainframe, software, or application, ancillary support equipment, telecommunications, energy/power/utility, etc.)

Communication and Information Management

Emergency management and incident response activities rely upon communications and information systems that support the formation of a common operating picture to all command and coordination sites. NIMS describes the requirements necessary for a standardized framework for communications and emphasizes the need for a common operating picture. NIMS is based upon the concepts of interoperability, reliability, scalability, portability, and the resiliency and redundancy of communication and information systems. When inspecting this criterion, the following subcategories should be considered: common operating picture, interoperability, scalability, plain language, and information security. Assessors will respond to questions in each area.

NIMS is scalable to any situation from small, local events to large-scale incidents, whether pre-planned, forewarned, or no-notice. This scalability is essential for NIMS to be applicable across the full spectrum of multiple agency, multiple jurisdiction, Statewide, and National events.

Resource Management

When inspecting resource management applications, three subcategories should be considered: preparedness, incident response, and post-incident recovery and reimbursement.

The preparedness activities (resource typing, credentialing, and inventory) are conducted on a continual basis to help ensure that resources are ready to be mobilized when called to an incident. Resource management during an event/incident includes (requirements identification, ordering and acquiring, mobilizing, and tracking and reporting). Post-event activities include recovery/demobilization and reimbursement.

Command and Management

The Command and Management component within NIMS is designed to enable effective and efficient incident management and coordination by providing flexible, standardized incident management structure. The structure is based on three key organizational constructs: the ICS, Multiagency Coordination Systems, and Public Information. ICS is based on 14 proven management characteristics, each of which contributes to the strength and efficiency of the overall system (Reference the NIMS Document, Component IV – Command and Management, for additional information). Assessors will rate the product's applicability to each of the 14 management characteristics of ICS, as applicable.

Other Criteria – Implementation and Product Overview

It is important to understand the implementation factors including the time and training impacts on governmental entities. This is especially important for small and rural agencies, which may have limited resources. While specific product costs are typically negotiated at the time of sale, vendors are asked to provide an estimate of product costs during the evaluation.

Step 2 – Apply Inspection Criteria and Complete NIMS STEP Worksheet

The second step in this review is to gain familiarization with the product and to apply the Inspection Criteria. The test analyst will arrange training on the product or provide assessors with information on self-paced training, if applicable. The assessors will also have time allocated for use of the system to become familiar with the product's capabilities.

A sample NIMS STEP Worksheet is provided below. Assessors are to review the product based on their application of the Inspection Criteria. These reviews should be made according to a subjective inspection based upon the individual assessor's knowledge of NIMS and experience.

Step 3 – Address General Questions

The third and final step is to address general questions for the product. The questions focus on addressing potential issues that may arise during implementation. For each question, the assessor must provide a detailed answer focusing on the ESF that they represent.

NIMS STEP Worksheet

Assessors will use the following guidance to complete the NIMS STEP Worksheet:

- Disagree: The product is designed or intended to address the statement but the product is not consistent with the statement presented.
- Agree: The product is consistent with the statement presented.
- Not Applicable: The product is not designed or intended to address the statement presented.

Table A-2: NIMS STEP Worksheet

Product Name:	
EMERGENCY SUPPORT	
Criteria and Question	**Result**
EMERGENCY SUPPORT FUNCTIONS	
1. This product supports the following Emergency Support Functions:	Disagree/Agree/Not Applicable
a. Transportation	
b. Communications	
c. Public Works and Engineering	
d. Firefighting	
e. Emergency Management	
f. Mass Care, Emergency Assistance, Housing, and Human Services	
g. Logistics Management and Resource Support	
h. Public Health and Medical Services	
i. Search and Rescue	
j. Oil and Hazardous Materials Response	
k. Agriculture and Natural Resources	
l. Energy	
m. Public Safety and Security	
n. Long-Term Community Recovery	
o. External Affairs	
2. There are no obstacles to ESF(s) implementing this product (i.e., from acquisition and installation to user proficiency).	
3. Provide comments on ESF(s) implementing this product.	

INCIDENT COMMAND	
4. This product supports the following Incident Command functions:	Disagree/Agree/Not Applicable
a. Incident Command	
b. Operations Function	
c. Planning Function	
d. Logistics Function	
e. Finance/Administration Function	
f. Intelligence/Investigations Function	
g. Public Information Function	
h. Safety Function	
i. Liaison Function	
5. There are no obstacles to Incident Command functions implementing this product.	
6. Provide comments on Incident Command functions implementing this product.	

HAZARDS	
Criteria and Question	**Result**
7. This product may be used in response to the following hazard types:	Disagree/Agree/Not Applicable
a. Natural Hazards	
b. Manmade Hazards	
8. Provide comments on Hazards applicability.	

COMMUNICATION AND INFORMATION MANAGEMENT	
Criteria and Question	**Result**
COMMON OPERATING PICTURE	
	Disagree/Agree/Not Applicable
9. This product provides adequate access to critical information:	
10. This product allows on-scene and off-scene personnel to have the same information about the incident, including the availability and location of resources and the status of assistance requests. (e.g., situational awareness).	
11. This product offers an incident overview by collating and gathering information (such as traffic weather, actual damage, resource availability) that enables the Incident Commander (IC), Unified Command (UC), and supporting agencies and organizations to make effective, consistent, and timely decisions.	
12. This product has the capability to be updated continually in order to maintain situational awareness.	
13. This product uses geospatial information pertaining to geographic location and characteristics of the incident.	
14. Provide comments on the common operating picture.	
INTEROPERABILITY	
	Disagree/Agree/Not Applicable
15. Incident reporting and documentation procedures are standardized to ensure that situational awareness is maintained and provides emergency management/response personnel with easy access to critical information.	
16. This product allows NIMS ICS forms to be completed.	
17. Provide comments on ICS forms.	
18. This product provides a method for data sharing or is interoperable with other incident management systems via voice, data, or video, etc.	
19. Provide comments on data sharing.	

SCALABILITY	
	Disagree/Agree/Not Applicable
20. This product may be used for small scale incidents and events.	
21. This product may be used for large scale incidents and events.	
22. This product may be used across the full spectrum of multi-agency incidents and events.	
23. This product may be used across the full spectrum of multi-discipline incidents and events.	
24. This product allows the responders to increase the number of users on a system.	
25. The product may be used at the following:	Disagree/Agree/Not Applicable
a. On scene as a portable or static device.	
b. On scene at the Incident Command Post (ICP).	
c. At a Staging Area, Base, or Camp.	
d. At a State or Local Department Operations Center (DOC) (any discipline).	
e. At a Local EOC.	
f. At a State EOC.	
g. At a Federal Joint Field Office (JFO) or EOC.	
26. Provide comments on Command and Coordination levels.	
27. This product may be used by multiple levels of government(s).	
28. This product may be used by the following levels of government:	Disagree/Agree/Not Applicable
a. Municipality	
b. County	
c. Tribal	
d. State	
e. Federal	
f. Special District	
g. Agency	
h. Other	
29. Provide comments on levels of government.	

30. This product is flexible enough to be used by the public and private sectors.	
31. Provide comments on scalability.	
PLAIN LANGUAGE	
	Disagree/Agree/Not Applicable
32. This product adheres to the principle of plain language (clear text).	
33. Provide comments on the use of plain language.	
INFORMATION SECURITY	
	Disagree/Agree/Not Applicable
34. The product provides a means to properly authenticate and certify users for security purposes.	
35. The product provides adequate controls to restrict access to sensitive information.	
36. This product does not have potential security or vulnerability concerns.	
37. Describe any safeguards integrated to minimize security and/or vulnerability concerns.	
38. Provide any additional comments on information security.	

RESOURCE MANAGEMENT

Criteria and Question	Result
	Disagree/Agree/Not Applicable
39. This product addresses the need to manage resources.	
40. This product allows for the inventorying of resources.	
41. This product identifies the use of personnel and equipment under mutual-aid agreements.	
42. This product provides for the inventorying of FEMA typed resources.	
43. This product provides for the inventorying of non-FEMA typed resources.	
44. This product has a built-in redundancy capability as a part of its functionality.	
45. The product addresses the use of mutual aid resources.	
46. This product allows for personnel accounting.	

47. This product provides a record of credentialed personnel.	
48. This product provides for accessing credentials/certifications of personnel.	
49. This product provides a record of other personnel.	
50. This product provides for resource requesting/ordering.	
51. The product provides for acquiring resources.	
52. This product provides for resource tracking/reporting.	
53. This product provides for resource recovery/demobilization.	
54. This product provides a reimbursement process.	
55. Provide comments on resource management.	

COMMAND AND MANAGEMENT

Criteria and Question	Result
	Disagree/Agree/Not Applicable
56. This product assists users in the management of an incident.	
57. This product supports (or is consistent with) the following management characteristics of ICS:	Disagree/Agree/Not Applicable
a. *Common Terminology*	
b. *Modular Organization*	
c. *Management by Objectives*	
d. *Incident Action Planning*	
e. *Manageable Span of Control*	
f. *Incident Facilities and Locations*	
g. *Comprehensive Resource Management*	
h. *Integrated Communications*	
i. *Establishment and Transfer of Command*	
j. *Chain of Command and Unity of Command*	
k. *Unified Command*	
l. *Accountability*	
m. *Dispatch/Deployment*	
n. *Information and Intelligence Management*	

58. The organizational charts and/or terminology used in the product are consistent with Incident Command.	
59. Comment on the products integration of management characteristics of ICS.	
IMPLEMENTATION AND PRODUCT OVERVIEW	
Criteria and Question	**Result**
IMPLEMENTATION	
	Disagree/Agree/Not Applicable
60. This product can be easily implemented.	
61. Comment on implementation.	
62. System documentation (including training materials and user's guides) is comprehensive.	
63. The vendor provides the following types of practitioner training:	Disagree/Agree/Not Applicable
a. Online	
b. Train the trainer	
c. On-site presentation	
d. Hands-on training	
64. Comment on practitioner training.	
65. Training provided allows recipients to proficiently use this product.	
66. There are no obstacles that would prohibit a department or agency from providing the training to implement this product?	
67. Describe any obstacles to training.	
68. This product has an integrated help tool.	
69. Comment on help tool integration (is it adequate/intuitive?).	
70. Is customer support available? If so, what is its availability and what medium is used (e.g., e-mail, phone, live-chat)?	
71. How long would it take a department or agency to implement this product?	
72. The size or make up of the department or agency will affect the implementation of this product.	
73. Comment on any identified impacts.	
74. Federal, state, or local laws or regulations will not hinder the implementation of this product.	

75. Comment on any laws that may hinder this implementation.	
76. The impact of implementing this product will not vary for urban vs. rural jurisdictions.	
77. Identify any issues with urban vs. rural implementation.	
78. The impact of implementing this product will not vary for paid, combination, or volunteer departments.	
79. Identify any issues with paid, combination, or volunteer departments.	
80. Provide an estimate of the cost of this product (optional).	
81. Provide an estimate of associated costs that may be incurred in addition to the procurement of this product (staffing, etc.).	
PRODUCT OVERVIEW	
82. Overall, this product is consistent with the concepts and principles of the NIMS.	
83. Identify any issues with NIMS consistency.	
84. This product will enhance the user's ability to do his/her job.	
85. Comment on how this product will impact the job performance for the user.	
86. This product was easy to use and intuitive.	
87. Comment on the products ease of use.	
88. This product was reliable during the evaluation.	
89. Describe any issues with reliability.	
90. Provide any other observations.	

NIMS STEP

Assessor Program

The National Preparedness Directorate (NPD) has developed a program to assist responders identify products that adhere to national interoperability standards and the concepts and principles of the National Incident Management System (NIMS).

The program, called the NIMS Supporting Technology Evaluation Program (NIMS STEP), provides objective evaluations of supporting technologies. Evaluation activities are designed to expand technology solutions, and provide the emergency response community with a comprehensive process to assist in the purchasing of information technology.

The NIMS STEP Assessor Program aims to involve state and local emergency management officials and responders in the evaluation program. Their involvement is intended to provide insights into responder needs and real-world applications and challenges associated with information technology. Officials that participate as an assessor learn about new incident management technologies, and gain an understanding of interoperability standards and NIMS concepts for the benefit of their jurisdiction.

Assessors will work as part of a team to evaluate new and emerging technologies within their discipline/response field. Participants will need to be available up to four days, depending on the complexity of the product under evaluation. Although some evaluations may be conducted remotely, most take place at the NIMS Support Center (NIMS SC) in Somerset, Kentucky. The NIMS SC will reimburse volunteers for allowable travel, meal and incidental costs.

State and local emergency managers and responders are encouraged to apply for an assessor position by visiting the program website at: www.nimsstep.org or by contacting staff at: nimsstep@nimssc.net.

Assessor Qualifications:

Each evaluation relies on the participation of qualified personnel that meet the following minimum qualifications:

- Five or more years of experience in emergency management, response or recovery.
- Experience in responding to real-world incidents.
- Experience using incident management software systems during exercises and/or real world incidents.
- Completed the following courses: IS-100, IS-200, IS-700, IS-800B and ICS-300.
- Proficient in basic Microsoft Office applications and capable of clearly documenting findings.

APPENDIX C: FEDERAL PARTNERS AND THE NIMS SC

National Preparedness Directorate, FEMA

The 2006 Post-Katrina Emergency Management Reform Act mandated the creation of the NPD, unifying DHS' preparedness, mitigation, response, and recovery missions. Established on 1 April 2007, the NPD oversees the coordination and development of the capabilities and tools necessary to prepare for terrorist incidents and natural disasters. The NPD provides strategy, policy, and planning guidance to build prevention, protection, response, and recovery capabilities among all levels of government throughout the Nation.

The National Integration Center (NIC), a division of the NPD, is responsible for developing, managing, and coordinating all homeland security training, education (external), exercise and lessons learned programs, as required, to ensure the Nation is prepared to prevent, protect against, respond to, recover from, and mitigate all hazards, natural or manmade. The IMSI Division, situated within the NIC, oversees response policy by maintaining, revising, and disseminating the NIMS, the NRF, and related materials. The IMSI Division oversees all aspects of NIMS including the development of compliance criteria and implementation activities at federal, state, and local levels. It provides guidance and support to jurisdictions and incident management and responder organizations as they adopt the system.

DHS Science and Technology Directorate

The NIMS STEP works closely with DHS's Test & Evaluation and Standards section. The Test & Evaluation and Standards section works across DHS and ensures that systems meet the capability needs of users, validates performance and provides measurable improvement to operational capabilities. Effective testing and evaluation programs provide crucial information to decision makers for acquisition and deployment of technology.

The NIMS STEP also collaborates with DHS's Command, Control and Interoperability Division. Their mission is to transform new and promising concepts into real operational capabilities. The Division is working with Federal partners to strengthen communications interoperability, improve Internet security and integrity, and accelerate the development of automated capabilities to help identify potential national threats.

NIMS Support Center

To support NIMS implementation, DHS established the NIMS SC in 2005 – a program that operates under a Cooperative Agreement between the FEMA and the Justice and Safety Center/Eastern Kentucky University (EKU). EKU has two strategic partners – Science Applications International Corporation (SAIC) and G&H International Services (GHIS) – that provide the NIMS SC with a variety of capabilities in support of NIMS implementation. The NIMS SC provides direct support to the IMSI Division.

The NIMS SC is designed to develop new emergency responder tools, enhance technology integration, and evaluate and report on products and standards to improve incident management and information sharing throughout the responder community. The program provides products and services in the following areas:

- Systems Development
- Standards and Test & Evaluation
- Technical Assistance and Incident Management Support

For additional information about the NIMS SC, please call or e-mail the staff at:

E-mail: FEMA-NIMS@dhs.gov
Phone: 202-646-3850

APPENDIX D: NIMS TECHNOLOGY EVALAUTION AND STANDARDS WORKING GROUP – FY 2009

Background

Pursuant to HSPD-5, the DHS created the NIMS in 2004. NIMS establishes a national framework to facilitate collaboration among all relevant organizations in preparing for, protecting against, responding to, and recovering from the entire spectrum of all-hazard events.

According to NIMS, "[c]ommunications and data standards, related testing, and associated compliance mechanisms are necessary to enable diverse organizations to work together effectively (NIMS – December 2008)." To promote the integration of standards and NIMS concepts among incident management products, the FEMA NPD established NIMS STEP. This program provides a mechanism for testing supporting technologies – the use and incorporation of new and existing technologies to improve efficiency and effectiveness in all aspects of incident management. The NIMS SC manages the day-to-day functions of the program under the direction of the NPD's IMSI Division.

Another fundamental responsibility of the NPD is to identify standards that will help emergency managers and responders organize effective responses to incidents and planned events. To this end, incident management standards development efforts are monitored and tools such as case studies and smart practices are developed to provide assistance to practitioners. The NIMS Technology Evaluation and Standards Working Group (Working Group) is formed to provide the IMSI Division with input into these respective task areas.

Objectives

NIMS STEP:

- Make recommendations on enhancements to all aspects of the NIMS STEP program.
- Review and provide input into process documentation (e.g., guidance materials, report templates, assessor materials) for the NIMS STEP program.
- Make recommendations regarding the NIMS STEP website.
- Identify a member to represent the Working Group on the Product Selection Committee.
- Make recommendations regarding hardware and software tools that would strengthen/support the test and evaluation process (i.e., simulation tools, communications devices and interfaces, etc.).
- Review feedback provided by vendors following the evaluation (e.g., post-evaluation questionnaires, informal "hotwash" comments).

- Review feedback provided to the NIMS STEP team from other sources.
- Identify venues for outreach and participate in outreach activities, as appropriate.
- Represent the emergency response community and areas of technical and operational expertise.

Standards:

- Identify and evaluate communication and information management standards that support NIMS.
- Review and provide input into standards-related outreach materials in order to help communicate how selected standards support NIMS and benefit the field.
- Represent the emergency response community and areas of technical and operational expertise.

Membership

The Working Group represents a cross-section of stakeholders representing various emergency response disciplines, the test and evaluation community, as well as SMEs for the selected information sharing standards. Specifically, members are identified and selected based on their knowledge of interoperability issues and experience purchasing and using incident management technologies. The composition of the Working Group generally reflects the following disciplines/areas of expertise:

1. State NIMS Coordinator
2. Emergency Management (Technical Representative)
3. Fire (Technical Representative)
4. Law Enforcement (Technical Representative)
5. Public Health/Emergency Medical Service (EMS)/Hospital (Technical Representative)
6. Geographic Information Services(GIS)/Modeling and Simulation Technology Specialist
7. Purchasing/Grants Management Official (State or local level of government)
8. Vendor Representative
9. Standard SME (Participant with expertise in a specific communication or information management field)
10. Standard SME (Participant with expertise in a specific communication or information management field)

11. Additional Public Safety Representative or Standard SME

12. Additional Public Safety Representative or Standard SME

Federal officials and NIMS SC staff may serve on the Working Group in an Ex Officio capacity. Specifically, test and evaluation officials from DHS' Science and Technology Directorate (most notably the Test and Evaluation and Standards Division and the Command, Control, and Interoperability Division) will be invited to participate on all Working Group activities.

APPENDIX E: VENDOR CONSENT FORM

A vendor consent form will be coordinated with the vendor during the evaluation planning process. Vendors should apply using the forms available online (http://www.nimsstep.org).

Vendor Consent Form

In order to participate in the NIMS STEP, vendors must sign the following consent form. By participating in the program, vendors provide their consent to the IMSI Division regarding the posting of the results/report for public viewing. In the event that significant technical or operational issues surface prior to the evaluation, the team will advise the vendor. The vendor will then have the option to perform corrective actions, begin the evaluation without taking corrective actions, or withdraw from the evaluation. Once the evaluation begins, the vendor will not be permitted to withdraw.

By signing this form, I agree to the aforementioned terms and have read and agree to the policies outlined in this NIMS STEP Guide, dated April 2009.

Signature: ______________________________

Name (printed): ______________________________

Title: ______________________________

Date: ______________________________

Address: ______________________________

____

____

Telephone No.: ______________________________

APPENDIX F: REFERENCES

1. OASIS Standard CAP-v1.1, October 2005.

2. OASIS Standard EDXL-DE v1.0, May 2006.

3. OASIS Standard EDXL-HAVE v1.0, November 2008.

4. OASIS Standard EDXL-RM v1.0, November 2008.

5. National Incident Management System, December 2008.

6. National Response Framework, January 2008.

7. NFPA 1600: Standard on Disaster/Emergency Management and Business Continuity Programs, 2007.

8. NIMS Recommended Standard List, http://www.fema.gov/library/viewRecord.do?id=3139 January 2008.

APPENDIX G: ACRONYMS AND ABBREVIATIONS

A2LA	Association for Laboratory Accreditation
ANSI	American National Standards Institute
CAP	Common Alerting Protocol
CBEFF	Common Biometric Exchange Formats Framework
DCS	Data Collection System
DHS	Department of Homeland Security
DMIS	Disaster Management Interoperability Services
DOC	Department Operations Center
EDXL	Emergency Data eXchange Language
EDXL-DE	Emergency Data eXchange Language – Distribution Element
EDXL-HAVE	Emergency Data eXchange Language – Hospital AVailability Exchange
EDXL-RM	Emergency Data eXchange Language – Resource Messaging
EKU	Eastern Kentucky University
EOC	Emergency Operations Center
EMS	Emergency Medical Service
ESF	Emergency Support Function
FEMA	Federal Emergency Management Agency
FY	Fiscal Year
GHIS	G&H International Services
GIS	Geographic Information Systems
HSPD	Homeland Security Presidential Directive
HTTP	Hypertext Transfer Protocol
IC	Incident Commander
ICP	Incident Command Post
ICS	Incident Command System

IEC	International Electrotechnical Commission
IEEE	Institute of Electrical and Electronics Engineers
IMSI	Incident Management Systems Integration
INCITS	InterNational Committee for Information Technology Standards
IS	Independent Study
ISO	International Organization for Standardization
IT	Information Technology
JFO	Joint Field Office
N/A	Not Applicable
NDA	Non-Disclosure Agreement
NFPA	National Fire Protection Association
NGO	Non-Governmental Organizations
NIC	National Integration Center
NIMS	National Incident Management System
NIMS SC	National Incident Management System Support Center
NIMS STEP	National Incident Management System Supporting Technology Evaluation Program
NPD	National Preparedness Directorate
NRF	National Response Framework
OASIS	Organization for the Advancement of Structured Information Standards
OPEN	Open Platform for Emergency Networks
QC	Quality Control
RFP	Requests for Proposal
RKB	Responder Knowledge Base
RSL	Recommended Standards List
SAIC	Science Applications International Corporation
SME	Subject Matter Expert
SOAP	Simple Object Access Protocol

T&E	Test and Evaluation
UC	Unified Command
XML	eXtensible Markup Language

www.ingramcontent.com/pod-product-compliance
Lightning Source LLC
Chambersburg PA
CBHW080619290526
45790CB00007B/2840
* 9 7 8 1 4 8 2 5 1 2 0 0 7 *